About
GLASTONBURY

POLLY LLOYD

BOSSINEY BOOKS

First published in 1992
by Bossiney Books,
St Teath, Bodmin, Cornwall.

Reprinted in 1994, 1997
by Penwell Print Ltd, Callington, Cornwall.

ISBN 0948158 78 6

ACKNOWLEDGEMENTS
Front cover photography: ROY WESTLAKE.
Back cover photography: JULIA DAVEY.
Other photographs: RAY BISHOP; ROSEMARY CLINCH.
Drawings: FELICITY YOUNG (page 31, 33, 35);
          GLYNIS MASSEY (pages 6, 7, 12, 77).
Front cover design: MAGGIE GINGER.

The original Hatherell paintings on pages 38 and 39 can be seen at the Halls of
Chivalry, Tintagel, North Cornwall.

THE RUINS of Glastonbury Abbey attract ▶
thousands of visitors every year.

ABOUT THE AUTHOR and THE BOOK

POLLY LLOYD, who lives in Bristol, is well-known on Westcountry radio and television.

She made her debut for Bossiney in 1988 with Legends of Dorset. *In 1989 she wrote* About Exmoor, *and in 1991 she was co-author of* Somerset Mysteries. *She has also written a chapter in* Wiltshire Mysteries. *She recently made a television documentary on domestic violence on BBC2. She was also on the Steering Committee of FeM FM, Britain's first all-women radio station which broadcast in Bristol during the 1992 International Women's Festival.*

Polly Lloyd is a considerable all-rounder: a gifted communicator through radio and television and a thoughtful, perceptive writer. She may write about legends but she has the wit and wisdom to know that there is no such thing as pure myth, and equally she understands that real people can – and do – become living legends. Talking and travelling with her is invariably a worthwhile experience, and such is the quality of her writing that we, the reader, can somehow travel by proxy.

Her harvesting can be of contrast: she can research deeply or, like the genesis of a Daphne du Maurier story, it can be something observed, something overheard, a whole theme triggered. In the media she has interviewed all types and temperaments: politicians and poets, cricketers and crackpots, actresses and aldermen, vicars and victims. Consequently she can sense – almost scent – the phoney, but she probes with good manners, and, like Sue Lawley or Anna Ford, she retains a sense of objectivity.

In this, Bossiney's 208th title, Polly Lloyd explores Glastonbury. Joseph of Arimathea, the Holy Thorn, Chalice Well, the Saints, King Arthur, the Glastonbury Zodiac and Glastonbury Tor are just some of the subjects featured on her tour. The author thoughtfully concludes '. . . Glastonbury today perfectly reflects this blend of past, present and future, the known and the unknown, the fact and the legend.'

ACROSS THE Abbey grounds the view stretches to the Tor – the combination of Abbey ruins, the Tor with its magic and mystery, its unfailing spring water and its atmosphere of folklore and fantasy, continues to draw visitors of all persuasions to Glastonbury.

ABOUT GLASTONBURY

NEARLY TWO thousand years ago a man came to England to spread the word of Christ. He chose to settle at the foot of a strange hill, and there he built a tiny church, dedicated to the Virgin Mary. In time the church grew to be one of the most powerful and influential abbeys in England. Saints lived and worshipped here, kings were crowned and buried here.

One great king, much loved for his courage and gallantry, fought many battles close by and eventually saved his country from the invader. Mortally wounded, he was carried here and threw his sword into the river. Throughout his life he had searched for the Holy Grail, and some believe the Grail lies hidden here still.

At the height of its glory, the Abbey fell victim to another king who, having turned against Rome, destroyed all the great abbeys in England.

The Abbey was in ruins but the strange hill continued to draw people to it. Spring water flowed unfailingly from its slopes, and flows still, and each year at Christmas a thorn tree blossomed in the Abbey grounds, and continues to do so.

For all its strong links with Christianity, other philosophies flourish here. Someone has found the signs of the zodiac traced out in the landscape. The hill seems to have a mystical power which some recognise as part of an ancient order as yet unnamed, a knowledge and understanding that have been forgotten but wait to be rediscovered.

People come to the strange hill and the town below it to admire the past, to enjoy the present and to consider the future. This is Glastonbury.

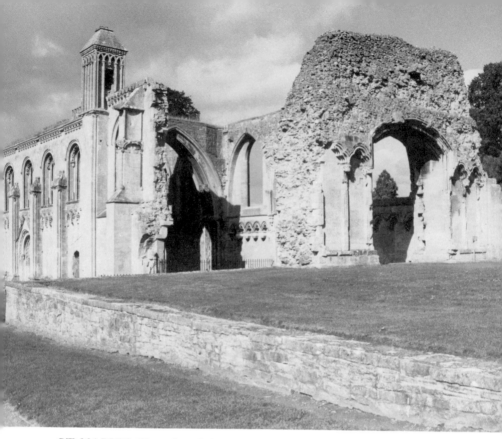

ST MARY'S Chapel and the Galilee – perfect proportions and elegant stonework, seen here against a storm-laden summer sky.

JOSEPH OF ARIMATHEA

IN THE legends and traditions of Glastonbury and in the history of the British Isles, Joseph of Arimathea played a very important role. He is credited with bringing Christianity to these shores, founding the first Christian church in 63AD.

Joseph of Arimathea is believed to have been the uncle of the Virgin Mary. He is mentioned in each of the four Gospels. St Matthew refers to him as 'a rich man . . . who also was Jesus's disciple', St Mark says he was 'a councillor of honourable estate, who was also himself looking for the kingdom of God'. St Luke records that Joseph of Arimathea was 'a good man and righteous' and St John writes that he was 'a disciple of Jesus but secretly for fear of the Jews'.

It was Joseph who asked Pilate for permission to take the body of Christ and bury it in a tomb. He and Nicodemus lifted the bruised and bleeding body of Jesus gently from the Cross and anointed it with a mixture of myrrh and aloes, and wrapped it in clean linen. Together they took the body to a nearby place, a garden, to a tomb which had not been used before – Joseph's own tomb, according to St Matthew, which he had hewn out of rock. And there they laid Christ's body, sealing the doorway with a huge boulder.

Joseph is said to have collected a few drops of the blood and sweat of Christ in two silver cups or cruets. He is also believed to have kept the cup or chalice which Jesus used at the Last Supper to demonstrate the sacrament to his disciples. In fact some scholars believe the Last Supper took place in Joseph of Arimathea's house. The two cruets and the chalice went with Joseph on his travels, destined to become linked inextricably with the legends of Glastonbury.

WEARY ALL HILL.

HERE ON Weʹaryall Hill, in 1800, John Clark erected a memorial stone to record the arrival of Joseph of Arimathea.

The disciples journeyed far from the Holy Land to spread the gospel, each to a different destination. Joseph of Arimathea accompanied St Philip to Gaul, and some years later moved on with a small party of followers to Britain. Now some people believe he had visited Britain before, that he was a tin trader who came to the West Country for Cornish tin and lead from the Mendip hills. There is also speculation that he might have brought his nephew Jesus with him, a line of thought which inspired William Blake to ask, in his great hymn 'Jerusalem':

And did those feet in ancient time
Walk upon England's mountains green?
And was the holy Lamb of God
On England's pleasant pastures seen?

Whether this was Joseph's first visit or not, he travelled to Glastonbury, apparently bringing with him the silver cruets and the chalice. Pausing to rest on Wearyall Hill, he plunged his staff into the ground where it miraculously took root and grew into a thorn tree which blossomed at Christmas. The group of twelve, including Joseph and his son Josephes, settled at Glastonbury. The King Arviragus gave them twelve hides of land tax free. The land is mentioned in the Domesday Book. There they built the first Christian church in Britain, a small wattle and daub construction dedicated to the Virgin Mary. According to tradition, it is the site on which the Abbey's Lady Chapel was later built. In the 1500s Abbot Richard Beere dug out a crypt under the Lady Chapel naming it St Joseph's Chapel and creating a shrine to Joseph of Arimathea. Richard Beere also created a new coat of arms incorporating a cross made from a sprouting staff and two cruets or cups.

Joseph's simple church was known as the Vetusta Ecclesia or Old Church and survived for many centuries before being destroyed in the great Abbey fire of 1184.

As for the Holy relics which Joseph brought with him, the two cruets are supposed to have been buried with him. Again the exact location of his grave is unknown although an ancient text attributed to Melkin, an early mystic or magus who lived 'before Merlin' says Joseph was buried on a forked line close to the southern corner of his

JOSEPH of Arimathea pauses to rest on Wearyall Hill. Here his staff miraculously took root in the ground and blossomed – the first Holy Thorn of Glastonbury.

TRADITIONALLY, Joseph of Arimathea, as a tin trader, visited England on several occasions and many believe the Boy Jesus accompanied him. This banner, depicting such a visit and with Glastonbury Tor in the background, hangs in Pilton Church.

wattle church. It goes on to add that when Joseph's tomb was found and opened it would be seen to be whole and untouched, and that from then on, neither water nor dew from heaven would fail those who inhabited the most noble island.

Some people see this as a reference to the Chalice Well, which has never run dry.

As for the Chalice itself, this has yet to be found, but it has become synonomous with the Holy Grail, an integral part of the Arthurian Legends and a symbol of the timeless quest for truth. And the story of Joseph of Arimathea, and his life in Glastonbury can be seen as pivotal to both the Christian and legendary aspects of the place that has been called 'this holiest earth'.

THE TRANQUIL peace of the Abbey grounds.

THE HOLY Thorn in the Abbey grounds, which flowers each Christmas. There are other thorn trees in Glastonbury, including one in St John's parish church.

15

THE HOLY THORN

THE HOLY Thorn of Glastonbury is said to have grown from the staff of Joseph of Arimathea. Joseph had journeyed to England with a small band of about eleven others to spread the word of Jesus. He travelled to Glastonbury and pausing to rest on Wearyall Hill he stuck his staff into the ground where it miraculously took root and began to sprout. Furthermore it blossomed at Christmastime.

It is an immensely powerful symbol, encompassing both the Christian and the mystical elements that make Glastonbury a magnet for pilgrims in search of a truth.

Although the Glastonbury thorn has its origins in the very earliest days of Christianity in Britain, the first reference to it does not appear until the sixteenth century. In 1520 a poem entitled 'The Lyfe of Joseph of Aramathea' was published which mentions

Thre hawthornes also, that groweth in Werall
Do burge and bere grene leaves at Christmas
As fresshe as other in May, when the nihtyngale
Wrestes out her notes musycall as pure as glas.

Some time before *The Lyfe of Joseph* appeared, Abbot Richard Beere, one of the most important heads of Glastonbury Abbey, adopted a new coat of arms. It can be seen in a stained glass window in St John's parish church. It consists of 'a green cross raguly with blood drops and cruets', that is, a cross of green sprouting wood flanked by two cruets or cups such as Joseph of Arimathea is said to have used to collect the blood and sweat of Christ, the whole covered with drops of blood. It would seem to be an obvious allusion to

GLASTONBURY Thorn photographed on Wearyall Hill in 1984.

THE IDENTIFYING notice by the Holy Thorn in the church.

both the Holy Thorn and the Holy Grail, although a firm link between the Holy Thorn and St Joseph's staff is a later addition to the legend. But clearly the Thorn had become an important symbol, or at the very least an object of curiosity. In the 1530s a Dr Layton, sent by Cromwell on behalf of Henry VIII to investigate the country's monasteries prior to the Dissolution wrote to his master:

By this bringer my servant I send you reliquaries; first, two flowers wrapped in white and black sarcenet that on Christmas Eve, hora ipsa qua Christus natus fuerat, will spring, and burgeon and bare blossoms . . .

And William Turner, twice Dean of Wells in the second half of the sixteenth century, compiled a 'Herbal' which includes this reference under the heading *'Of Oxycantha:'*

In Summerset shyre about six miles from Welles in the park of Gassenbury there is an hawthorne which is grene all the wynter as all they that dwell there about do stedfastly hold.

The Thorn has been used more than once to prove a point. In 1645 John Eachard, a clergyman, claimed it proved that December 25 was indeed Christ's birthday. In his *Good News for all Christian Soldiers* he wrote:

I know that England doe keep the right day that Christ was born on, above all the nations of Christendome, because we have a miracle hath often been seen in England upon that day, for we have a tree in England, called the Holy Thorne, by Glassenbury Abbey, nigh the Bathe, which on the 25 day of December, which is our Christmasse Day, hath constantly blossomed.

Charles I, when given a spring of blossom from the Holy Thorn, remarked that the tree obviously followed the old style calendar – Protestant England refused to accept Pope Gregory XIII's reform in 1582. England eventually fell into line in 1752, by losing eleven days; the following January the Somerset Evening Post told its readers:

A vast concourse of people attended the noted Thorn on Christmas Day, New Style, but to their great disappointment there was no sign of it blowing, which made them watch it narrowly the 6th January, the Christmas Day, Old Style, when it blowed as usual.

The link between Joseph of Arimathea and the thorn seems to have been made relatively late in the famous tree's history but once established took a firm hold on the public imagination. Some say the tree grew not from Joseph's staff but from a thorn he had taken from the cruel crown of thorns with which Jesus was taunted at his crucifixion, others say that Joseph's staff was made from the same wood as that infamous crown. The latter could well be true because the Holy Thorn at Glastonbury has been identified as *Crataegus oxycantha praecox* or *Crataegus monogyna* which can be found in the Holy Land. The original tree on Wearyall Hill no longer exists, although it seems to have been there until the second half of the eighteenth century. In 1800 John Clark erected a memorial stone inscribed '*JA Anno D XXXI*' to record Joseph of Arimathea's arrival in Britain. There are accounts of attempts to destroy the tree – during the reign of Elizabeth I a Puritan tried to chop it down. Apparently he managed to sink the axe into his leg by mistake and furthermore a flying splinter of wood blinded him in one eye. Later a Roundhead attacked the tree – he too came off rather badly.

Today there is more than one Holy Thorn. Cuttings have been

propagated and thrive in Westcountry gardens, and indeed have been sent further afield to America and Europe. The two most important however are the one in the Abbey grounds and the one that stands in front of St John's parish church*. There is also one by the Chalice Well. Custom dictates that a spray of blossom, traditionally cut by the Mayor from the tree at St John's, is sent to the Queen and the Queen Mother to decorate the Royal breakfast table on Christmas day.

The Glastonbury Thorn is one of the most famous and best-loved trees in England. For some it is merely a tourist attraction, a freak of nature that has been used to intrigue visitors. To others it is a powerful symbol that encompasses both the Christian and the mythical aspects of Glastonbury. For those who believe that it did indeed sprout from Joseph of Arimathea's staff it is a very real link through the centuries to Jesus Christ. Whichever one of the theories appeals most, to see it blossom in the bleak midwinter is to see a quintessential part of the enigma of Glastonbury.

---

* Early in 1992 the thorn in St John's Churchyard had to be cut down but it will be replaced by a younger thorn planted elsewhere in the churchyard.

ST JOHN'S parish church with its fine tower dates back to Norman times. The Glastonbury Thorn, to the right of the picture had to be cut down in 1992, but another, younger thorn tree in the churchyard will take its place.

THE CHALICE WELL

THE CHALICE Well has played an important role for centuries in the legends of Glastonbury. On a practical level, it was Glastonbury's main supply of fresh water until the nineteenth century and as late as 1921-22 saved the town from drought. The spring has never failed; 25,000 gallons of water flow from it every day. Its source is unknown. Possibly it originates in the Mendips, or even in South Wales. The water is crystal clear, but it does contain iron and this has turned the stone over which it flows a deep red, adding strength to the legends that surround it. Indeed, it is also known as the Blood Spring.

Excavations carried out by the archaeologist Philip Rahtz in 1961 uncovered some interesting facts. The spring had been covered by a well head and a pentagonal chamber which were presumably constructed above ground but which have now been completely covered with the passage of time. The well shaft is thought to date from the twelfth century, possibly from stones rescued from the Abbey which suffered a disastrous fire in 1184. The chamber next to it is later, possibly built around 1750 with more recent additions. Its exact purpose is uncertain although it may have been built as a type of sedimentation tank to clean the water.

Rahtz also discovered flints and shards of pottery dating from the Iron Age, as well as finds from Roman and medieval times. The stump of a yew tree was found which had obviously grown and died at that exact spot and scientific tests have shown that it would have grown in Roman times. This tells us that the ground level at that time lay approximately where the bottom of the Well is today so that we can assume that the spring came out at ground level in Roman

THE CHALICE Well. The wrought iron lid was designed by the architect Frederick Bligh Bond, the first director of excavations of the Abbey after its sale in 1907. The design is deeply symbolic, with reference to both Eastern and Western philosophy.

times. Interestingly, the yew tree grew in line with some other yews still growing near the Well, and with yet more lower down the slopes. The trees may have marked an ancient pathway used perhaps for rituals and ceremonial processions by the Druids who founded a college of instruction in Glastonbury.

According to tradition, Joseph of Arimathea and his followers settled nearby, building the first Christian shrine in Britain more or less where the ruins of St Mary's Chapel in the Abbey are today. The earliest baptisms were celebrated at the spring, and it became linked in people's minds with Joseph. He, of course, is said to have brought with him the Chalice or cup used by Jesus at the Last Supper, the search for which has become synonymous with the quest for the Holy Grail. Some say the Chalice is buried close by the spring, and this is how it got its name but the facts are somewhat hazy. In the thirteenth century the spring, or well, was known by a number of different names based on Chalcsell – Chalcwell, Chalscwellestrete, Chakwelle and Chalkwell. Since 1265 the main road which runs past the well has been called Chilkwell Street, but when Chalice Well became the accepted name is a mystery.

The first person to claim the water had healing properties was a Dr John Dee in 1582, who declared he had discovered the Elixir Vitae. Dr Dee was quite a character, a mathematician and an astrologer who apparently uncovered the Glastonbury Zodiac in 1580. Sadly for Dr Dee, no one took much notice of him on either count and another 350 years passed before Katharine Maltwood's investigations into the Zodiac, which you can read about elsewhere in this book, attracted public attention.

As to the beneficial properties of the spring, in the mid-eighteenth century, when taking the waters was the height of fashion, Glastonbury enjoyed its share of fame. In 1750 a man called Matthew Chancellor of North Wootton near Wells claimed he had been told in a dream to drink the water at Glastonbury on seven consecutive Sundays to cure his asthma. This he did – it worked and Matthew declared himself 'recovered of his disorder'. The news spread like wildfire and visitors flocked to Glastonbury. The Pump House, built in 1750, in Magdalene Street, and the Bath House, became hugely popular attractions. Crowds of people travelled from Bath and Bristol and surrounding areas and Glastonbury was literally full to overflowing. There simply were not enough lodgings to accommodate them all. On one day alone, May 5 1751, ten thousand people came to take the waters. Many of them claimed to have been cured and a list of testimonies sworn before a magistrate to be true and genuine was published in a book. Deafness, blindness, ulcers and the King's Evil were among the ailments named.

Eventually, of course, the excitement died down and the crowds disappeared, although people still drink the water, and find comfort and healing in Glastonbury.

Today the Chalice Well is surrounded by a beautiful garden. The

THE LION'S Head at the Chalice Well gardens, where visitors can drink the water that unfailingly flows. ▶

A SECLUDED corner of the Chalice Well Gardens: – a quiet moment.

THE LOWER part of the Chalice Well Gardens. ▶

water fills both parts of the wellhouse – the shaft and the chamber – and then flows through an underground pipe to re-emerge at the top of a waterfall in an area known as King Arthur's Court. A separate pipe carries a supply directly to the Lion's Head from which visitors can drink, with an extra pipe continuing to Wellhouse Lane so that water is available even when the gardens are closed. Meanwhile, the waterfall cascades into King Arthur's Court and flows into what was once the Pilgrim's Bath where many are said to have been healed, then underground again to the circular pools in the lower part of the garden. After that, the spring joins other underground streams and goes on to the Abbey grounds.

The well head is covered with a wrought iron lid designed by Frederick Bligh Bond who was an architect and the first director of excavations at the Abbey after its sale in 1907. It was given in 1919 in thanks for peace after the Great War by Friends of Glastonbury. The design is deeply symbolic with reference to both Eastern and Western philosophy, to ancient design and Christian belief. The two

interlocking circles can be seen in earthworks and structures throughout the world, and can also be connected to the Sacred Geometry of Glastonbury Abbey. Early Christians adopted the central oval to symbolise the sacred fish and called it the Vesica Piscis. The particular design on the well lid is based on a thirteenth century pattern which represented the Bleeding Lance holding in balance the Visible and Invisible worlds locked together. It can also be interpreted as representing the Yin and the Yang, the conscious and unconscious and the blending of the masculine and feminine natures. Simple and graceful, it captures the essence of many philosophies.

The design is reflected in the two circular pools at the lower end of the gardens, the first one turbulent, the second one still and calm, representing between them the vitality of the spring and the stillness of the well, busy consciousness and thoughtful subconscience.

The garden itself is quite beautiful, filled with colour, scent and shape, changing with the seasons. The Chalice Well Trust, founded in 1958 by Wellesley Tudor Pole, is responsible for its care. It is a place for contemplation and quiet conversation, peaceful and calm, with the Tor rising up behind it. Here the visitor can leave the worries and cares of the outside world behind, soothed by nature and beauty, as the path winds from one area to the next, climbing gently to the well itself. It is a perfect setting for one of Glastonbury's great treasures.

GLASTONBURY SAINTS

THE LIST of pious and devout men and women associated with Glastonbury is long, as might be expected of a religious centre of such significance and status. And that list includes a number of saints dating back to the very earliest days of Christianity in Britain. St Gildas, St Kea and St Collen; the Celtic saints Benignus, Indract, Brigit, Columba and David, the patron Saint of Wales; St Neot and St Aethelwold from Anglo-Saxon times – all these saints have connections with Glastonbury. But there are three in particular whose lives merit special attention: St Joseph of Arimathea, who featured in an earlier chapter, St Patrick and St Dunstan.

According to legend, St Patrick was the first Abbot of Glastonbury. He had earlier been sent by Pope Celestine to Ireland where he converted the Irish people to Christianity, an act which caused him to be chosen as their special, patron, saint. From there he set sail for England and travelled to Glastonbury, arriving in about 433.

There he found a small group of devout men, twelve in number, living as hermits close by the tiny church which Joseph of Arimathea had built. This had been the tradition since Joseph himself had arrived in England. Patrick taught these men to live as a community, to work and pray together, and in return they chose him as their leader, the first in a long and illustrious line of Abbots. And from this small beginning grew the powerful structure of Glastonbury Abbey.

St. Patrick's remains were buried to the right of the High Altar, a position of great honour which reflected his importance. After the Great Fire of 1184 he was reburied in a stone pyramid or obelisk covered in silver and gold, which soon became an important shrine.

This is the legend of St Patrick, but as with so many elements of

THE CHURCH of St Benedict, or Benignus. Benignus was a pupil of St Patrick, said to be the first Abbot of Glastonbury and became Abbot himself after St Patrick's death.

Glastonbury's history, the facts are a little hazy. Certainly, Glastonbury does seem to have held a great attraction for Irish visitors. The name of nearby Beckery is derived, according to some scholars, from words meaning 'Little Ireland'. But whether these Irish pilgrims came to Glastonbury because St Patrick had lived there, or whether the legend of St Patrick's connection grew simply because there were so many Irish visitors is not clear.

Much of the story is based on St Patrick's Charter, a thirteenth century manuscript which influenced many later historians. In it, St Patrick relates his own story, his time in Ireland and his journey to Glastonbury. But current thinking dismisses the Charter as, at worst, a thirteenth century forgery, at best, an over-enthusiastic misinterpretation of an earlier document.

There is even a suggestion of a second St Patrick. Some scholars believe there is evidence that he lived around the same time as Ireland's patron saint and suggest it was this second St Patrick who came to Glastonbury. Whatever the truth – and it is unlikely that it

ST PATRICK travelled to Glastonbury …

can ever be proved conclusively one way or the other – the Irish connection was a strong one. Patrick was succeeded as Abbot by his disciple St Beningnus, or Benedict, who has a church named after him in the town. And St Brigit spent a number of years worshipping at the chapel dedicated to St Mary Magdalene at Beckery, leaving behind some important relics including her purse and a bell. This bell, incidentally, is reputed to have belonged to Miss Alice Buckton, the playwright and last private owner of the Chalice Well, but has since disappeared. Two carvings of St Brigit can still be seen, one on the tower of St Michael's on the Tor, the other at St Mary's.

If there are those who would cast doubts on St Patrick's association with Glastonbury, there can be no denying the role played by St Dunstan. Once again, the history of the Abbey is intertwined with the history of country, underlining the importance of Glastonbury.

St Dunstan was a remarkable man, intelligent, articulate, talented, wise and courageous. Such a combination can prove dangerous and there were some who resented Dunstan's influence at the Royal Court and set about removing him. But Dunstan, as we shall see, won through in the end.

Dunstan was born at Baltonsborough, not far from Glastonbury, in 909, the year in which Athelm, to whom he was related, was consecrated the first bishop in Somerset. Dunstan was introduced to the court of King Athelstan in 925 and soon found favour. Before long, this caused trouble and Dunstan was forced to flee. He went to the Bishop of Winchester, another relative, who persuaded him to go abroad and spend some time at a Benedictine monastery. This proved to be a turning point for Dunstan who recognised an ideal in the Benedictine regime that influenced him for the rest of his life. Eventually, he returned to Glastonbury, initially as a hermit, building for himself a tiny cell just five feet by two and a half. Legend has it that the Devil came to tempt him, but Dunstan recognised him and, seizing him by the nose, threw him out.

This pious existence, however, did not last too long and Dunstan began to think that he might do more good from a position of influence at court. Athelstan had been succeeded by his brother Edmund who was equally impressed by Dunstan's ability. Once again his success made him enemies who managed to turn the King against him, and once again Dunstan was forced to flee. This time however the

THE DEVIL came to tempt him, but Dunstan recognised him and seizing him by the nose, threw him out!

King saw the error of his ways, in a most dramatic fashion. Edmund was out hunting on Mendip when his horse bolted and galloped full speed to the very edge of Cheddar Gorge. In those few moments as he faced certain death, Edmund realised he had treated Dunstan badly and repented. Miraculously his terrified horse immediately stopped and Edmund was saved. Convinced that this was divine intervention, he wasted no time in arranging a reconciliation with Dunstan – in fact he made him Abbot of Glastonbury and promised to pay for some improvements to the Abbey.

It was the start of a period of great success for Dunstan. With support from the Crown, firstly Edmund and later Eadred, the Abbey flourished. Dunstan developed the Rule of St Benedict, a guide for spiritual and material direction with its vows of poverty, chastity and obedience. The movement began to spread throughout the country, establishing structure and stability and encouraging growth and rebuilding. But it was perhaps inevitable that a man of Dunstan's forthright character should run into trouble again and it happened when Aedred died in 955 and was succeeded by Eadwig.

Eadwig was a very different person from his predecessor. Where Eadred had trusted Dunstan to the extent that he ordered the Royal Treasury and Archives to be moved to Glastonbury, and was happy to listen to Dunstan's advice and counsel, Eadwig was more independent. He and Dunstan clashed from the very beginning – his coronation.

Eadwig had become bored with the ceremony and celebrations and upset everyone by walking out. Dunstan was appalled by such disregard for duty and went in search of the new king. He found him in his private apartment – with the royal crown cast carelessly to one side. This was too much for Dunstan who picked up the crown, stuck it on the king's head and marched him back into the banqueting hall.

This was not the way to treat a new king, especially one as headstrong as Eadwig, and once again Dunstan found himself in exile. He spent the time in Ghent studying European monasteries and there he might have been expected to stay for the rest of his days.

But the story continues. In 957 Dunstan was recalled by Eadwig's younger brother Edgar, king of Mercia, who made Dunstan Bishop of Worcester. Eadwig's death had opened the door for a united king-

HIS HORSE bolted and galloped full speed to the very edge of Cheddar Gorge …

dom under Edgar and after just a few years, Dunstan found himself Archbishop of Canterbury. He continued to be a strong influence with the king and when Edgar died he was buried at Glastonbury.

Dunstan was to crown two more kings – Edward the Martyr and Ethelred. He gave his final sermon on Ascension Day in 988, knowing his life would soon be over, and he died peacefully on May 19 988.

The importance of Dunstan and his contribution, not only to his Abbey, but also to his country, cannot be over-emphasised. A man of great personal charisma, he was a talented musician, illuminator and designer, crafts which became an integral part of life at the Abbey. His wisdom and learning earned him the respect of kings and consequently he was able to influence affairs of state. His teaching and his belief in the Benedictine Rule were the cornerstone of a great community at Glastonbury and under his guidance the Abbey flourished. This duel role of statesman and cleric gave him the sort of power and status we see reflected in the lives of Becket and Wolsey, for example. Dunstan set high standards and taught his followers well.

It is no coincidence that four Glastonbury monks went on to become Bishops of Wells during the tenth century and of the six Archbishops of Canterbury who followed Dunstan himself, five were from Glastonbury and one was related to him. The history of Glastonbury Abbey is filled with clever and pious men, but St Dunstan must surely rank as one of the most outstanding.

ARTHUR

'THE KING had sent word to the great Abbey. He had heard a travelling singer prophesy that the body would be found in a hollowed oak sixteen feet below the ground. He wanted the monks to uncover it and reveal the truth. In the shelter of the Abbey walls, charred and blackened by the recent catastrophic fire, the brothers dug away the earth. It was hard, slow work, but at last, at a depth of sixteen feet, just as the bard had predicted, they found the hollowed oak. And within it lay two skeletons, one male, one female. A lock of golden hair still clung to the woman's skull; the man, tall and broad, had ten wounds to his head. And buried with them was a lead cross inscribed in Latin:

Hic jacet sepultus inclitis rex Arthurus cum Wenneveria uxore sua secunda in insula Avallonia.

Arthur and Guenevere, buried in Avalon.'

The story of Arthur, Britain's greatest warrior, and his queen Guinevere, is one to capture the imagination, to quicken the heart and stir the blood. His great battles, his courage and chivalry, his knights and his famous Round Table are the stuff of legends, recounted time and again both in England and abroad. Arthur was a hero held very dear.

And yet, unlike Alfred, another great king whose Westcountry battles shaped the future of Britain, Arthur still remains very much a mystery, to the extent that some historians dispute his very existence. The story of the discovery of his body at Glastonbury Abbey

ANOTHER ARTHURIAN painting from Hatherell – Sir Galahad entering Camelot.

around 1190 is found in an account by the historian Giraldus, written soon after the event and probably the 'official' version. But many modern scholars dismiss the whole thing as a hoax, perhaps instigated by King Henry II who had his own reasons for wanting to prove for once and for all that Arthur was dead and buried, not some immortal champion who would return one day to lead his people again. And the Abbey itself was in desperate need of some new attractions to bring in the pilgrims because the great fire of 1184 had destroyed so many of the holy relics and treasures that drew people to Glastonbury. Certainly both parties stood to gain enough to make faking the discovery a worthwhile risk.

◀ *ARTHUR RECEIVES the sword Excalibur from the Lady of the Lake. The painting is by Hatherell.*

EXCALIBUR, symbolised at Taunton.

Trying to unravel the story of Arthur is a fascinating but frustrating business. The early chroniclers of British history give conflicting accounts. Nennius, who wrote in the early ninth century, describes Arthur as the leader of the Britons in war, which could mean anything from a petty general to a mighty king. He tells of Arthur's twelve battles and says he died in 539. Arthur excelled himself at the battle of Badon, single-handedly slaying almost a thousand of the enemy, according to Nennius, and other historians acknowledge Badon as a crucial battle, although they do not always agree on its exact location. But Gildas, who was born in the year of that battle, makes no mention whatsoever of Arthur in his account.

Fact merged with legend early on. When William of Malmesbury wrote his *Deeds of the Kings of England*, circa 1125, there were already two versions of Arthur, a factual one and one of mythical proportions. William believed the facts were enough to earn Arthur great respect as a man who put cohesion and backbone into a crumbling weary nation. He regretted that the mystery surrounding Arthur's final resting place had given strength to the legend that Arthur would return – *rex quondam, rexque futuris* – the king that was, the king that shall be.

Much of the responsibility – or blame – for the legend of Arthur lies with the twelfth century historian Geoffrey of Monmouth whose version of events brings together all the elements now associated with him. He writes about Arthur succeeding to the throne and rallying his people against the Saxons, of his great battles – including Badon – and his mighty sword Excalibur. After defeating the Saxons, Arthur overcame the Picts and the Scots, and then married his beautiful queen Guinevere. Abroad he conquered Ireland and Iceland, and then Norway, Denmark and Gaul. Small wonder news of his feats spread far and wide. His next challenge was Rome but at this point his treacherous nephew Mordred tried to take the throne for himself and Arthur had to return home to deal with him. They met in battle near the river Camlon in Cornwall and Arthur beat Mordred but was himself mortally wounded and carried back to Avalon.

These are the bare bones of the story. The rich detail of Arthurian legends includes Merlin, Lancelot and Morgan la Fey, the Round Table and the search for the Holy Grail. It is a story that has intrigued countless people for centuries, and which has parallels in the ancient sagas of other cultures. The fable is well known, the facts remain elusive. Cornishmen will tell you that Arthur belongs to Tintagel, not Glastonbury. Others place Camelot in Wales or even Winchester. The site of the decisive battle of Badon is disputed too – some say it was Cadbury Camp but others disagree. It is a debate that will doubtless continue.

But let us return to the discovery of the bodies of Arthur and Guinevere. Their remains were reburied in 1278 in a black marble tomb in front of the high altar at Glastonbury Abbey. King Edward I and Queen Eleanor were present at the ceremony. The tomb was lost after the Dissolution, but the site was rediscovered during excavations in 1934 and today it is clearly marked. It is enough to confirm in many people's minds that Arthur's final resting place was indeed Glastonbury, the ancient Isle of Avalon.

There is, however, another highly romantic version of Arthur's death. After his bitter battle against the evil Mordred, Arthur, by now mortally wounded, was carried back to Avalon on a barge. He still had with him his trusted sword Excalibur and when he reached Pomparles Bridge, which is midway between Glastonbury and Street, he flung it into the water. And then Arthur himself was carried away 'by unknown persons or by the Lady of the Lake with promise to bring him back again one day.'

So what is truth and what is legend? And which is more important? It is hard to accept that Arthur never existed at all; the legend is too strong, the evidence, although muddled, is too persuasive. On one point all the early historians who wrote about Arthur are agreed: he was a great leader of men. He was the embodiment of everything that is noble and valiant and honest. And if the story has gained something in the telling, no matter. Arthur is still a hero for all times.

The twelfth century chronicler Wace understood this well. He wrote:

. . . truth has turned to fable and an idle song . . . The minstrel has sung his ballad, the storyteller told over his tale so frequently, little by little he has decked and painted, till by reason of his embellishment the truth stands his in the trappings of a tale. Thus to make a delectable tune to your ear, history goes masking as fable.

ARTHUR'S WELL at Cadbury, which some say is the site of his most decisive battles.

GLASTONBURY ZODIAC

ONE OF the most intriguing of Glastonbury's many mysteries lay hidden in the landscape for centuries before being uncovered in the 1920's by a remarkable woman called Katharine Maltwood. Even today, some people dismiss it as a figment of an overactive imagination but others regard it as evidence of a long lost knowledge.

It is called the Glastonbury Zodiac and is quite literally that – a giant zodiac with the twelve astrological signs drawn out within a circle some ten miles in diameter, perfectly aligned to reflect the stars they represent. The symbols are outlined by lanes and streams, with woods and hedges and the natural contours of the land adding detail.

Katharine Maltwood was a sculptor who exhibited at the Royal Academy. She had a keen interest in mystical matters which was often reflected in her work and in the early 1920s she began to study the Arthurian legends. At about the same time, a publishing company asked her to illustrate a new translation of a Norman-French manuscript called *The High History of the Holy Grail*. This was reputedly written many centuries ago at Glastonbury Abbey and chronicles the journeys of knights in search of the Grail. Reading the text in preparation for her illustrations, Katharine began to recognise familiar places, places which she felt sure could be found in the Vale of Avalon.

Her imagination was fired, and while plotting out the journeys of the knights she began to realise she could make out the shape of a huge lion. Its belly was outlined by the River Cary, its back by Somerton Lane, an ancient road. Her next discovery was the figure of a man. Katharine was intrigued but at a loss to find an explanation.

THE GLASTONBURY ZODIAC.

1. ARIES. THE RAM.
2. TAURUS. THE BULL.
3. GEMINI. THE TWINS.
4. CANCER. A SHIP (MODERN SYMBOL IS A CRAB).
5. LEO. THE LION
6. VIRGO. THE VIRGIN
7. LIBRA. A DOVE (MODERN SYMBOL IS THE SCALES).
8. SCORPIO. THE SCORPION
9. SAGITTARIUS. THE CENTAUR.
10. CAPRICORN. THE GOAT
11. AQUARIUS. A PHOENIX (MODERN SYMBOL IS THE WATERBEARER).
12. PISCES. THE FISHES. (MODERN SYMBOL IS TWO FISHES BUT THIS
ZODIAC HAS ALSO INCLUDED A WHALE.).

A conversation with an astrologist friend provided the key to the puzzle. Could the lion and the man represent the astrological signs of Leo and Gemini? Before long Katharine had mapped out all twelve signs, a perfect zodiac hidden in the Somerset countryside around Glastonbury. The horns of Taurus the bull stretch out from Hatch Hill, the Scorpion's tail stings the rump of Sagitarrius' horse at Withial, the back of Capricorn the goat is marked by the road from Glastonbury to Shepton Mallett.

In 1935 Katharine published her theory in a book entitled *Glastonbury's Temple of the Stars*. Not surprisingly cynics greeted it with derision. How could such features remain unchanged for centuries in a continually changing landscape? Who directed the pattern of lanes and hedges? Who could possibly outline figures too large to be seen clearly, other than from the air? Katharine and her followers stood firm. An unseen hand had guided the men who made the roads and laid the hedges. Furthermore, they believed it was possible to tie in the Glastonbury Zodiac with the great legends and sagas – the Celtic bards and the Norse storymen for instance. King Arthur himself has been linked with the zodiac – he being identified as the sign Sagitarrius and the zodiac representing the Round Table. Even the names of local villages, farms and inns, and nearby landmarks, such as hills and lanes are interconnected.

The historian Geoffrey Ashe believes Nostradamus was referring to the Glastonbury Zodiac when he wrote: *In the land of the great heavenly temple A nephew at London is murdered through a false peace* – the nephew being the Duke of Monmouth whose army was defeated at nearby Sedgemoor and who was subsequently beheaded by his uncle, James II. Other scholars have pointed to Stonehenge and other stone circles, to megalithic monuments and ley lines as indications that early man had a knowledge and understanding of geometry and astronomy far more sophisticated than might be imagined, traditions that were lost centuries ago and are only now beginning to be rediscovered.

Arguments about the Glastonbury Zodiac will no doubt continue, watched by a crowd of open-minded interested onlookers. It can be argued that those who believe in the Glastonbury Zodiac are halfway to seeing all sorts of ill-defined phenomena. There is a singular lack of hard evidence and a notable readiness to accept ambiguity, to jump to easy conclusions. But if it is true, it is one of Britain's biggest antiquities, dazzling in its complexity.

Astrologically speaking, today we are on the verge of the Age of

1. ARIES   THE RAM.
21st MARCH to 21st APRIL.

2. TAURUS.   THE BULL.
21st APRIL to 21st MAY.

3. GEMINI.   THE TWINS
21st MAY TO 21st JUNE.

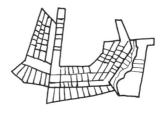

4. CANCER.   THE CRAB (OR SHIP).
21st JUNE To 21st JULY.

5. LEO.   THE LION.
21st JULY to 21st AUGUST

6. VIRGO.   THE VIRGIN
21st AUGUST TO 21st SEPTEMBER

GLASTONBURY Zodiac Signs.

7. LIBRA. THE SCALES (OR DOVE).
21st SEPTEMBER TO 21st OCTOBER.

8. SCORPIO. THE SCORPION.
21st OCTOBER TO 21st NOVEMBER.

9. SAGITTARIUS. THE CENTAUR.
21st NOVEMBER TO 21st DECEMBER.

10. CAPRICORN. THE GOAT.
21st DEC. TO 21st JAN.

11. AQUARIUS. THE PHOENIX
(OR WATERBEARER).
21st JAN. TO 21st FEB.

12. PISCES. THE FISHES.
21st FEB TO 21st MARCH.

▲ *GLASTONBURY Zodiac Signs – the Tor forms the head of the phoenix in Aquarius.*

THE TOR, rising between the stark winter trees. ▶

Aquarius, the New Age whose philosophies are already being embraced by many people. In the Glastonbury Zodiac the sign of Aquarius is represented by a phoenix which carries with it a feeling or re-birth, of new beginnings. And as Katharine Maltwood showed that sign of Aquarius lies over Glastonbury Tor.

Perhaps the least surprising aspect of this great mystery is the fact that it belongs to Glastonbury, home to so many unexplained mysteries.

GLASTONBURY TOR

SEEING Glastonbury Tor for the first time brings a feeling of instant recognition, like seeing an old friend, because somehow it seems so familiar. It is a famous image, this strange hill such as a child might draw, crowned with a ruined church tower. It stands like a beacon in the Vale of Avalon, attracting visitors like a magnet. It changes its appearance as one approaches; from some angles it looks quite stark and lonely, from others softer and more a part of the Somerset countryside. Travelling towards it on the Shepton Mallet road it is very imposing and darkly powerful, seen from the Abbey grounds it looks far more reassuring. The light too changes its character, the late sun bathing it in gold, the shadows of dusk painting it purple, the moonlight shining silver on its dark contours. And when the mists roll in off the Levels leaving only the tower visible, like a finger pointing to the heavens, it seem to embody every mystical story ever told about Glastonbury.

Thousands of visitors every year climb to the summit, 520 feet above sea level, the steepness and the view combining to take their breath away. There is invariably a wind blowing around the Tor, sometimes quite strong, and it is an invigorating experience. On a clear day, of course, one can see for miles. And standing there on top of the world one cannot help but wonder what tricks of nature produced such an extraordinary place.

Such a prominent landmark would undoubtedly have attracted the very earliest settlers. Excavations of the famous Lake Villages at Meare and Godney, inhabited in the Iron Age, show that rubble from the foot of the Tor was used in their construction. The villages were eventually abandoned, probably because the land became flooded,

THIS VIEW of Glastonbury Tor shows the terraces quite clearly.

and there follows something of a gap in our knowledge of the Tor's history. But archaeological discoveries show that it was inhabited in the sixth century and judging by the quality of the fragments of pottery and the metalwork found there, the people who lived there were of some importance, perhaps a monastic community. Indeed it is quite possible that the Tor was a sacred place long before Christianity reached these shores, for the Lake villagers during the Bronze Age and as the archaeologist Dr Ralegh Radford suggests, by the Celts. There is a huge earthworks at nearby Ponter's Ball, pre-Roman, and he argues that this was not used as a military defence but as a sanctuary, a sacred place where Celtic Kings were buried. Its juxtaposition

THE TOR and its ruined chapel, dominate the Somerset countryside.

with the Chalice Well and the Tor fits a Celtic format. And places of religious importance, albeit pagan, were frequently taken over by Christians.

In Norman times a chapel dedicated to St Michael was built on the summit of the Tor but this was destroyed by an earthquake in 1275. Incidentally, this earthquake was by no means unique – Wells cathedral had been damaged by a similar tremor in 1248. The chapel was not rebuilt for another fifty years or so, when Adam of Sodbury was Abbot at Glastonbury. He achieved a good deal – apart from replacing the Tor chapel he also completed the vaulting of the nave in the Great church and dedicated two chapels to St Silvester and St George, as well as providing new bells and an organ for the abbey, and acquiring a number of treasures such as a beautiful bible, several important books, gold and silver ornaments and three sets of silk.

In the fifteenth century a tower was added to the west end of Adam's chapel, and it is this that remains today, a romantic ruin topping one of Somerset's most famous landmarks.

Given the rich catalogue of myth and legend associated with Avalon, it is hardly surprising that the Tor has its own share of mystery. The very fact that it dominates the landscape seems to imbue it with a certain power. To begin with, it stands on two ley lines. These are invisible lines linking prominent features at certain points; on a practical level they could be used as navigational aids, guiding the traveller from point to point across great distances, but on a more mystic level they are believed by some to represent a geometry whose meaning has been forgotten, or to indicate places where metaphysical forces are strongest. One of the two major ley lines that passes through Glastonbury runs from the Abbey to Stonehenge and on to Canterbury Cathedral, the other stretches from St Michael's mount off the Cornish Coast to the chapel on the Tor and on to the stone circle at Avebury in Wiltshire.

Any thoughts that the Tor might be man-made have long been dismissed, but there are those who believe there is a cave deep within it. Cracks in the rock at the summit were thought perhaps to indicate an entrance to such a cave but excavations carried out in 1964-66 by the

THE VIEW from the top of Glastonbury Tor makes the climb worthwhile.

A SERVICE at Glastonbury Abbey in 1909 attended by the Prince and Princess of Wales.

archaeologist Philip Rahtz drew a blank. A number of people closely associated with Glastonbury, such as Major Wellesley Tudor Pole, who sponsored Rahtz's excavations, and who founded the Chalice Well Trust, and Geoffrey Russell who put forward the so-called Maze Theory, firmly believed there was a cave within the Tor. Wellesley Tudor Pole accepted the lack of hard evidence very philosophically. He felt certain that a great discovery was waiting to be made, but that it was being saved for a future generation.

The Maze Theory, as suggested by Geoffrey Russell, has the same sort of appeal as Katharine Maltwood's Glastonbury Zodiac, which features in another chapter, and similarly is derided by those of a cynical nature and welcomed by those who are more accepting of the world's mysteries. An Irishman with a keen interest in the symbolism and significance of mazes and a well-informed understanding of the Arthurian legends, Russell made a study of the terraces that can be seen on the Tor. These are particularly clear on its north side. He concluded that they had been cut into the hillside by prehistoric man to form a maze. Mazes and labyrinths are found throughout the world in many different cultures and have a symbolism that goes far deeper than the idea of a network of hedged paths designed to do little more than entertain the idle rich. A true maze has a geometry and a symmetry, and represented, perhaps, a journey to God. It could be used as a path for penitents. It is made up of a number of pathways which are linked but do not overlap. The Tor maze has seven such pathways – so too did the famous Cretan Labyrinth. And at Tintagel, reputed to be the birthplace of Arthur, there is a carving of a maze believed to be 3,500 years old.

If Geoffrey Russell's theory is correct, then the Tor Maze is on a par with Stonehenge in terms of prehistoric engineering. It would mean that Glastonbury was an established centre of pagan worship – all the more reason for the early Christians to choose it as a site. It would add even greater weight to the importance of Glastonbury throughout the ages.

On the other hand, of course, the terraces might just be part of some agricultural scheme – a vineyard, perhaps. But that is the charm of Glastonbury. It offers fact, probability and speculation, and leaves the choice to us.

THE GLORY OF GLASTONBURY

THERE IS a serenity about the ruins of Glastonbury Abbey that has touched the heart of countless visitors. With the Tor rising behind them, the remnants of the ancient walls somehow manage to retain their grace and elegance. The ruins of the Great Church hold within them yet that soothing stillness that is found in places where men have worshipped their God for centuries.

The outlines of the cluster of Abbey buildings, traced in the neatly tended lawns, give a hint of times long gone. With a little imagination it is easy to picture how magnificent it must have been. But when people speak of the glory of Glastonbury, they are referring to more than a collection of beautiful buildings. For Glastonbury Abbey was once one of the greatest ecclesiastical centres in the country.

In order to appreciate the importance of Glastonbury in its heyday it is necessary to understand its role in society. The Church was a much more integral part of everyday life in the Middle Ages and ordinary people looked to the clergy for guidance and advice. Monasteries and abbeys were seats of learning as well as being religious centres, and Glastonbury had an excellent reputation with many sons of noblemen being sent there to be educated. The Abbey had a fine library filled with costly books, which dated back to the tenth century when St Dunstan, returning from exile abroad, encouraged the monks to teach and write and to produce books and manuscripts that were beautifully illuminated and illustrated. In matters of state, the church was hugely influential; as a consequence its bishops and abbots were powerful men. In particular Glastonbury seemed to be a favourite and through the centuries received many

THE SHEER size of this broken shell shows the magnificence of the Abbey.

benefits and a good deal of support from various kings. And spiritually Glastonbury was one of the greatest abbeys, possibly only St Albans was more important.

As well as power, influence and prestige, Glastonbury also had wealth. By the end of the eleventh century it already owned 41 manors which provided considerable financial security. By 1252, the Abbey census listed 892 oxen, 60 bullocks, 23 colts, 223 cows, 19 bulls, 153 heifers and young oxen, 26 steers, 126 yearlings, 6,717 sheep and 327 pigs, as well as enough wheat to see it through the winter. Such stability made Glastonbury a very attractive place. At the height of its glory, it could comfortably accommodate five hundred visitors, and when the Abbots themselves travelled it was with a retinue of at least one hundred. The part played by Glastonbury

Abbey was central not only to the area it served but to the country as a whole.

So how had this great powerhouse evolved from the tiny wattle and daub church that Joseph of Arimathea built? Each of the abbots played their part of course, and a succession of kings held influence over the Abbey, but some made their mark more boldly than others.

One of the Abbey's earliest benefactors was the Saxon king Ine. When the Saxons first invaded Britain, they were heathens who wrought havoc throughout the country and desecrated churches. Fortunately they never quite reached Glastonbury until after their king Cynegils was converted to Christianity. Ine became king in 688 and proved to be extremely generous to Glastonbury, granting it land and money and eventually building a new stone church dedicated to Saint Peter and St Paul. Ine was a man of vision whose aim was to unify the many churches and monasteries which were existing quite separately from each other. He wanted Glastonbury to take a leading role in this new united Church.

After many years as a great leader and warrior, Ine abdicated and together with his wife went to spend his final years in Rome, choosing a life of simplicity and piety. But before he went he gave Glastonbury two special privileges. Firstly, he made the Abbey independent of the bishops – something that was to irritate subsequent bishops of Bath and Wells for many a year – and secondly, he personally asked for, and received, papal protection for Glastonbury. These two factors paved the way for Glastonbury's future success.

Two centuries later, St Dunstan – whose story is told in another chapter – added to Ine's church. He made it longer and built a tower, as well as a number of other buildings. It was a time of re-building – the Danes had been vanquished and new churches were replacing the ones wrecked by the invader, and the abbeys and monasteries took up their old role as teachers. Glastonbury was part of this upsurge, and rapidly grew in importance. While Dunstan was Abbot he crowned no fewer than three kings – Edgar, Edward the Martyr and Ethelred.

After the Norman Conquest, the abbots of Glastonbury began to expand the Abbey. Thurston started work on a new church which Herluin promptly rebuilt on a grander scale. In 1126 Henry de Blois, one of the great builders, was made Abbot. The nephew of Henry I,

AFTER THE Abbey was closed it rapidly fell into ruin, not least because local people raided it and carried off quantities of stone for their own use. Many of the houses, cottages and farmbuildings around the area contain stone from the Abbey.

THE SPG Summer School visit Glastonbury in 1911.

A VIEW of the Abbey from an unusual angle.

ACCORDING to legend, Arthur was mortally wounded by his bastard son, the treacherous Mordred, at the battle of Camlann and carried secretly to Glastonbury, where he died and was interred in the hollowed-out trunk of an oak tree …

he was also Bishop of Winchester, but happily he was a man of great ability who set about improving Glastonbury Abbey not only in terms of its buildings and possessions, but also in terms of power and influence. He built a bell tower, chapter house, cloister, lavatory, refectory, dormitory, infirmary (with its own chapel) a brewery and stables. He donated many beautiful treasures, including tapestries, vestments, a silver cross and a banner woven with gold thread. And these lists are by no means exhaustive. Furthermore, he was a great collector of relics, which in those days served a dual purpose. As well as being sacred and holy objects which added to the credibility and standing of the Abbey, they attracted pilgrims who of course brought extra revenue to both the Abbey and the town.

But in 1184 disaster struck. A terrible fire destroyed practically the whole Abbey. Only a chamber and a chapel, and the bell tower built by Henry de Blois survived. The other buildings, the treasures, the books, the relics were all lost, and so tragically was the Old Church, revered by one and all as the first Christian church in Britain.

After the Great Fire work began almost immediately on the Church of St Mary – the Lady Chapel – and also on the Great church. Slowly but surely the Abbey grew again, helped no doubt by the timely discovery of the grave of King Arthur and Queen Guinevere, which attracted plenty of visitors at a time when money was a priority.

It was during the fourteenth and fifteenth century that the great building schemes took place, and the breathtakingly beautiful Great Church with its graceful vaulting became the centrepiece of one of the most important abbeys in England. Each of the Abbots added in some way to the glory of Glastonbury, including the great Richard Beere. He was a cultured man – he knew Erasmus – and he acted as ambassador for Henry VII. Beere was Abbot from 1493 to 1524 and in that time he began the Edgar Chapel, built a crypt under the Lady Chapel, which he dedicated to Joseph of Arimathea, built two other chapels and a church, and rebuilt the Tribunal, from where justice was administered on behalf of the Abbot. He also added extra vaulting and flying buttresses to the Great Church.

THIS SHIELD listing the Glastonbury Abbots hangs ▶
in the Abbot's Kitchen.

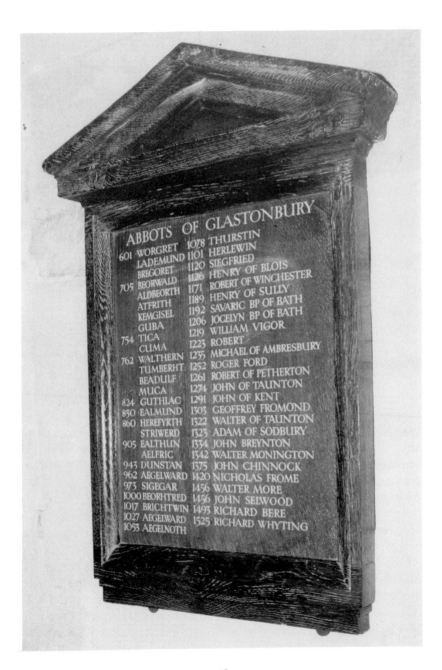

ABBOTS OF GLASTONBURY

601	WORGRET	1078	THURSTIN
	LADEMUND	1101	HERLEWIN
	BREGORET	1120	SIEGFRIED
705	BEORWALD	1126	HENRY OF BLOIS
	ALDBEORTH	1171	ROBERT OF WINCHESTER
	ATFRITH	1189	HENRY OF SULLY
	KEMGISEL	1192	SAVARIC BP OF BATH
	GUBA	1206	JOCELYN BP OF BATH
754	TICA	1219	WILLIAM VIGOR
	CUMA	1223	ROBERT
762	WALTHERN	1235	MICHAEL OF AMBRESBURY
	TUMBERHT	1252	ROGER FORD
	BEADULF	1261	ROBERT OF PETHERTON
	MUCA	1274	JOHN OF TAUNTON
824	GUTHLAC	1291	JOHN OF KENT
850	EALMUND	1303	GEOFFREY FROMOND
860	HEREFYRTH	1322	WALTER OF TAUNTON
	STRIWERD	1323	ADAM OF SODBURY
905	EALTHUN	1334	JOHN BREYNTON
	AELFRIC	1342	WALTER MONINGTON
943	DUNSTAN	1375	JOHN CHINNOCK
962	AEGELWARD	1420	NICHOLAS FROME
973	SIGEGAR	1456	WALTER MORE
1000	BEORHTRED	1456	JOHN SELWOOD
1017	BRICHTWIN	1493	RICHARD BERE
1027	AEGELWARD	1525	RICHARD WHYTING
1053	AEGELNOTH		

65

THE RUINS of St Mary's Chapel, showing the beautiful stonework. It was the first building to be completed after the Great Fire of 1184.

Beere was succeeded by Richard Whiting. The monks had asked Cardinal Wolsey to nominate him, a politically sound move, and they felt the Abbey was safe. There was a new king on the throne, but after all, he had been designated Defender of the Faith by the Pope so there seemed to be no cause for concern on that front. There was wealth, security and prestige, and the future looked golden.

No one could possibly have imagined the dark days ahead, but time was running out for Glastonbury. Henry VIII, for reasons more secular than spiritual, broke away from Rome. Wolsey was dead. Henry set about destroying the monasteries.

One by one the smaller establishments were sacked or persuaded to surrender, then Sir Thomas Cromwell, acting as the King's agent, gradually worked his way through the other ecclesiastical communities until only the biggest were left. Glastonbury was one of the last. It was a rich prize, as wealthy as Westminster Abbey. Its revenues would swell the royal coffers considerably. In September 1539,

Cromwell sent his commissioners to Somerset.

Abbot Whiting was staying at Sharpham Manor when they arrived. They demanded that he surrender the Abbey. Despite the fact that he was old and somewhat feeble, he bravely refused. They interrogated him, and searched the manor, looking for incriminating evidence. Eventually a book was found which criticised the King's divorce. Whether Cromwell's men really found it, or whether they planted it there is open to debate,. In any event, Whiting was charged with high treason. He was found guilty and sentenced to death.

The execution was particularly gruesome. Whiting, frail and elderly, was strapped to a hurdle and dragged through the streets of Glastonbury to the foot of the Tor. With him were John Thorne, the Abbey treasurer, and a young monk called Roger Wilfrid. It was a bleak November day, the wind as always whipping around the Tor. At the summit were three gallows. It must have seemed unbelievable to the people of the town and the Abbey that such a thing could be happening.

The old Abbot was led to the top of the Tor together with the two others and all three were hanged. But for Whiting there was more indignity to follow. When his body was cut down, it was beheaded and quartered. Then an order was given for each of the quarters to be taken to a different town – to Wells, Bath, Ilchester and Bridgwater – and displayed in a public place. His head was hung from the gateway of the Abbey itself.

And with the death of its last Abbot came the end of the Abbey. Its estates were broken up, its riches plundered. The birthplace of Christianity in Britain, the jewel in the Church's crown had survived fifteen centuries of threat from Saxons, Danes and Normans. It had kept its independence despite the attempts of various bishops and monarchs to overrule it. It had seen kings crowned and saints proclaimed and had grown to be one of the most architecturally beautiful and spiritually important places in the country. It had seemed that nothing could harm it.

But with that cruel and bloody execution on the Tor, the glory of Glastonbury ended for ever.

◀ *A CRUEL and bloody execution.*

ANOTHER WAY
OF LIFE

THE GRUESOME execution of Abbot Richard Whiting sig-
nalled the end of a way of life for both town and Abbey that had
developed over many centuries. The Abbey was the centre piece of
an ordered structure that governed people for miles around, its influence touching every part of their lives in some way or another. The
Abbot as head of the Abbey was in effect landlord, judge, teacher,
administrator and priest, and the Abbey was the heart of a large comfortable community. All this was lost for ever.

These days the Abbey grounds are a peaceful retreat from the
bustling town around them, but picture the buildings as they once
were and one begins to get an idea of how the Abbey must have
dominated the town. There is a detailed scale model of the Great
Church in the Abbey museum which illustrates its sheer size and
shows how it towered over the shops and inns in the High Street.
The destruction of the Abbey must have left a gaping wound in the
town on Glastonbury.

The decline of Glastonbury Abbey from greatness to ruin was dis-
turbingly rapid. It was soon stripped of all its treasures of course, but
the buildings themselves also proved too tempting to resist, and anything that could be taken away and used elsewhere was simply
removed. The lead was taken from the roofs, dressed stones were
carried off, timbers were cut away. A succession of owners seemed to
regard the building merely as a useful source of material. There was
no thought whatsoever of preserving it in any way; conserving his-
torical buildings is a relatively new concept.

After the death of Henry VIII, the man responsible for the Abbey's
downfall, his son Edward VI gave the ruins and grounds to the Duke

of Somerset, Edward Seymour, but when he fell from favour it reverted to the Crown. When the Catholic Mary came to the throne there were hopes that the Abbey might be reinstated. Four of the former monks wrote an impassioned plea to her, but Mary's reign was all too brief, and when Elizabeth, an ardent Protestant, succeeded her, these hopes were dashed. Elizabeth, in turn, gave the site to Sir Peter Carew and from then on until the early years of the twentieth century, the Abbey was privately owned.

In those long years the Abbey was used a couple of times by

THE ABBOT'S Kitchen in the Abbey grounds, fortunately preserved intact. For a while, after the Dissolution, it housed a group of Dutch weavers brought to England by the new owner of the Abbey, Edward Seymour, Duke of Somerset.

groups of people. Edward Seymour brought over a group of Protestant Dutch weavers whom he installed in the Abbot's Kitchen, and for a while they flourished. But they fled the country when Mary came to the throne and tried to re-impose Catholicism. And later, Quakers used the Kitchen as a place to hold their meetings – and probably ensured that it survived intact by doing so.

But for the most part the Abbey was cannibalised. Many a local building included stone from the Abbey. There are reports of carved stone, pillars, buttresses and the like being sold to the highest bidder. One owner even went so far as to use gunpowder to break down the walls to make it easier to carry the stone away. In some ways it is a miracle that anything was left at all. However there does seem to have been an idea that it was unlucky to use anything that came from the Abbey, fostered no doubt by the fact that the site never belonged to any one person for very long, and that ill fortune seemed to dog the various owners.

THE CHAPEL of St Patrick is the only intact chapel remaining at Glastonbury Abbey and dates back to 1512.

And so, perhaps more through superstition than respect for the Abbey, some locals refused to take anything. Others wary of tempting bad luck, but too practical to turn down a bargain, used the stone for their stables and outhouses, but not for their homes.

Some people, no doubt, did regret the destruction of the Abbey, but it was not until the nineteenth century that people really began to recognise that here was something worth saving. By this time of course there was very little left but attitudes were changing. In the second half of the century there was a revival of interest in all things medieval, and the legends of Arthur became very fashionable, so of course the romantic ruins of Glastonbury Abbey attracted a good deal of attention.

At the same time archaeologists were carrying out the first serious surveys of historic sites, academic and authoritative. Eventually in 1882 the Ancient Monuments Preservation Act was passed, designed to protect sites like Glastonbury, although it could be argued that the poetry of Alfred, Lord Tennyson, did as much to save the Abbey as the Act did. All in all the sad decline of Glastonbury Abbey through neglect and abuse was coming to an end, and a true appreciation of its beauty and importance would follow.

The turning point came in 1907 when the owner Stanley Austin announced that he wanted to sell the property. Stanley Austin was a wealthy man who lived in the Abbey House, almost directly opposite the offices of Austin and Bath, a firm of solicitors with whom he was a partner. Indeed Austin and Bath still practise in Glastonbury in the same premises in Chilkwell Street that they have occupied since 1840. I understand that they have in their possession a number of documents connected with the Abbey estate and its sale, including the Abbey wine cellar book of October 1896, and some correspondence with the Bishop of Bath and Wells.

An auction was arranged for the afternoon of Thursday 6 June, to be held in a marquee in the Abbey grounds at 3.30pm precisely. The auctioneer was Mr Robert Bowring from Wells, and naturally Austin and Bath looked after the legalities. A lavish sales brochure was prepared – there is a copy of it in the Abbey Museum – and a large crowd gathered to watch the proceedings.

There were two main bidders. One was Mr Ernest Jardine from

THE CRYPT under the Lady Chapel built around 1500.

Nottingham, who had made his money in the lace business, and who was at that time a prospective parliamentary candidate for East Somerset. The other was a mysterious American woman whose reasons for wanting to buy the Abbey are unclear. Some say she wanted to set up a 'School for Chivalry', others that she planned to present the Abbey to Roman Catholic Benedictines. Whatever her intentions she failed to reach Glastonbury in time, her train having been delayed, and arrived at the Abbey grounds to find that Ernest Jardine had bought the site for £30,000. Apparently she offered him more – and upped her offer again – but he refused to sell it to her, and the mysterious woman left.

Jardine had bought the Abbey on behalf of the Church of England. When the sale was announced the Bishop of Bath and Wells set about trying to raise enough money to buy it. He had secured about half by the date of the auction and he and Jardine made a gentleman's agreement that Jardine would act as a sort of holding agent, promising to sell it to the Church for the same price he had paid, once the Bishop had raised enough funds. Jardine was as good as his word and in 1908 ownership of the Abbey passed to the Bath and Wells Diocesan Trust, after 370 years in private hands.

One of the first steps taken by the new guardians of the Abbey was to appoint someone to take charge of proper excavations of the ruins. They chose Bristol architect Frederick Bligh Bond, a happy choice on the face of it because Bond was an expert on ecclesiastical architecture and was the author of a book on roodscreens and roodlofts. He also had a passion for Glastonbury.

Bond's work at Glastonbury lasted about a decade and during the course of it he made a number of important discoveries. For example, he outlined the two western towers, the north porch and many of the monastic buildings around the Great Church. He was particularly interested in the Edgar Chapel, built by Abbot Richard Beere, which lay behind the Great Altar. By his calculations, this added to the overall length of the Great Church, making it, at 594 feet, the longest church in England.

Bond was also one of the first people to suggest that there was a geometric significance to the dimensions of certain structures, particularly in Gothic architecture. It is a theory that has gained credence over the years and has been applied to a number of important constructions including Stonehenge, but at the time it was regarded with a good deal of scepticism.

Those who thought this aspect of Bond's work was somewhat eccentric were even more shocked to learn that he was communicating – or so he believed – with some of the monks who had lived at the Abbey centuries ago. Shortly after the sale of the Abbey, before his appointment, he had taken to visiting a medium who helped him get in touch with the monks, whom he referred to as the Brotherhood of Watchers or the Company of Avalon.

According to Bond, these monks had shown him the existence of the Edgar Chapel by means of automatic writing, that is to say, Bond's hand was guided by their spirits as he moved the pen across the paper.

Now it must be remembered that at the time Bond was working at Glastonbury there was a school of thought that believed in a sort of universal mind which could be reached on occasion by special people despite the obvious barriers of time and space. People like W.B. Yeats were fascinated by the idea of a collective consciousness that

THE PLAQUE reads: The cross, the symbol of our faith, the gift of Queen Elizabeth II, marks a Christian sanctuary so ancient that only legend can record its origin.

could be 'tapped into' and the philosophy was developed by Jung. Some people would doubtless regard it as perfectly natural for Bond's excavations to be directed by monks who had lived at the Abbey in bygone times.

Bond's employers, however, were appalled at the thought of someone with such unorthodox views working on behalf of the Church in a place of such religious importance. As the years went by, and Bond grew more convinced that he was in touch with the other side, relationships became strained. In 1917 he was dropped as Diocesan Architect, an honorary position he had taken up in 1909. Bond learnt about his dismissal by seeing the post advertised in a newspaper. The more he was criticised, the more firmly he clung to his ideas, and unfortunately he let standards slip as far as the excavations were concerned.

A split was inevitable and when, in 1922, Bond refused to work with a co-director appointed by the Somerset Archaeological Society, he was sacked.

One can quite appreciate that Bond's attitudes were simply not acceptable to the Diocesan Trust. But looking at his work from a more liberal, open-minded standpoint it seems to fit in so well with the idea of Glastonbury as a place where fact, myth and speculation blend together. Communicating with dead monks and drawing plans of the Abbey by means of automatic writing will be regarded as fanciful by many, but whatever way Bond was 'led' to the Edgar Chapel, it was an important discovery. His work had very real value in adding to our knowledge of the Abbey, and his ideas on the use of geometry and numerical perfection in the construction of buildings are no longer dismissed out of hand. For all his unorthodoxy, Frederick Bligh Bond fits in perfectly with the continuing story of Glastonbury.

ARCHITECT Frederick Bligh Bond, *chosen to lead the excavations after the Abbey was sold, believed he could communicate with former monks whose influence was transmitted via automatic writing.*

A COUNTRY TOWN

A S THE Abbey grew in size and importance, naturally the town of Glastonbury prospered. The Abbey provided plenty of work, everything from stonemasonry to farming. And of course there was a steady stream of visitors and pilgrims who all needed somewhere to sleep, stables for their horses, food and drink. The days of the Abbey's glory were halcyon days for the town of Glastonbury.

But because its good fortune was so dependent on the Abbey, the town suffered badly when Henry VIII's Dissolution reached Glastonbury. The unthinkable happened – the Abbey with all it represented was simply closed down and left to decay. And the horror of the barbarous execution of Abbot Whiting shook the community to its core. Virtually overnight a way of life that had taken centuries to develop, ended. The effect on the town must have been devastating. No more work from the Abbey, no-one to buy food and drink, no more wealthy visitors.

Think of the present-day communities we have seen decimated by the closure of pits or docks or factories – this is what happened to Glastonbury. Overshadowing the town was the decaying structure of the Abbey, gradually being pulled to pieces.

It is important to bear in mind the sheer size of the Abbey, especially the Great Church, and remember how it would have dwarfed the buildings clustered around it, and imagine what an ever-present reminder of past glories it would have been. These were hard and disruptive years for the Glastonbury, and it took a long time for the town to recover. As late as 1691 – more than a century later – the traveller Celia Fiennes wrote that it was *'a ragged place, very ragged and decayed'*.

But recover it did. The Abbey lands were divided up and sold, the buildings were pulled down and the stones re-used. Many a local house or stable had Abbey stone built into it. The old agricultural traditions continued and being Somerset there was plenty of cheese and cider. And sheep were important, with a growing trade in sheepskin. Things began to look up for Glastonbury.

By the start of the eighteenth century a number of industries had begun to establish themselves in the town. Textiles were important in Somerset, perhaps more than people realise, and Glastonbury's speciality was knitted stockings – for the Spanish trade, according to Daniel Defoe, writing in the 1720s. Silk was manufactured in Glastonbury from about 1793. And the town received a welcome boost in 1751 when a man called Matthew Chancellor claimed that the waters of the Chalice Well had healing properties. Taking the waters was very fashionable at the time, particularly at spars such as Bath, and Glastonbury was invaded by visitors anxious to try this new source. A new Pump Room and Bath House were built. The craze did not last long but nonetheless was welcomed by the townsfolk.

THIS postcard, sent in 1909, reminds us of the time when the Wells Old Road in Glastonbury was a tranquil country lane.

Glastonbury, Wells Old Road.

ANOTHER glimpse of old Glastonbury – the High Street.

During the nineteenth century two important events helped save Glastonbury from rural anonymity, by linking it with the outside world.

The first was the construction of the Glastonbury Canal which linked the town with the sea via the lower reaches of the River Brue, joining the sea at a tidal lock at Highbridge. Work started in 1829 and the canal opened on August 15 1833. At first it was a big success, not only providing a direct two-way route to transport goods quickly and easily, but also improving the drainage of the Brue valley. But its success was short-lived; the canal traffic was hampered by waterlogged peat which swelled up on the canal bed and blocked the way. Highbridge also began to suffer from silting problems.

But another more modern invention was on the way – the railway. In 1841 the Bristol and Exeter Railway Company opened a line between Bristol and Bridgwater which went through Highbridge. In 1848 the Company bought the Glastonbury Canal for £7,000 with firm promises to maintain it. Three years later the Somerset Central Railway Company was launched. It was given Royal Assent in June 1852 to begin work on a twelve-mile stretch between Glastonbury and Highbridge. The Bristol and Exeter, clearly recognising a white elephant, swapped the ill-fated Glastonbury Canal for shares in the new railway line. In 1845, twelve short years after its opening, the canal was closed.

Meanwhile there were great celebrations in Glastonbury for the first railway trip along the route. It marked progress and opportunity, a new era of industrialisation and better, swifter links with other towns and cities than had ever seemed possible. Interestingly, the board of directors who naturally were passengers on that first trip included James and Cyrus Clark who were to found one of the most important local industries – shoemaking. The railway went from strength to strength and in 1863 the Somerset Central joined forces with the Dorset Central to form the late lamented Somerset and Dorset – known affectionately as the Slow and Dirty. In 1890 a branch line was opened between Bridgwater and Glastonbury and

AND THE High Street in 1992 – the three sheep waiting patiently outside one of the shops proved, on closer inspection, to be stuffed!

this picturesque route through the Somerset countryside was much loved by generations of passengers who would watch out for a first glimpse of the Tor.

Work with sheepskin and leather played an important part in Glastonbury's history and in the 1800s it really took hold. Two famous names spring to mind – Morlands of Glastonbury and Clarks of Street, but with respect to Morlands, Clarks is the more important.

James Clark set up in business in 1825 as a 'fell-monger, skin dresser and maker of sheepskin rugs'. In 1833 his brother Cyrus went into partnership with him and began making wool-lined slippers. From these humble beginnings grew a huge shoe-making empire which now operates from a number of places, including a factory in Portugal, but still has a base at Street, just a stone's throw from Glastonbury and almost within site of the Tor, which for many years was used as their trademark.

Sheepskin still features strongly in Glastonbury. Walk down the High Street and you will see many shops selling rugs, jackets, bags and slippers made of soft, comfortable sheepskin. The traditional country crafts abound and there is plenty to choose from to take home as a souvenir. And like any country town there are antique shops to tempt the visitor too.

But where Glastonbury differs from other small towns is in the proliferation of shops which deal in what could loosely be described as New Age artefacts. Treasure troves of candles and crystals, strange carvings and colourful clothes. Shops filled with books on any number of religions and philosophies, myths and legends. And tiny places offering every kind of alternative – or complementary – medicine, from aromatherapy to shia-tsu massage, as well as tarot readings and astrology.

And it is because of this emphasis on the mystical that Glastonbury differs from any other small, attractive country town. The Abbey ruins alone are enough to attract visitors, but there seems to be more. Cynics may sneer, but many people can sense something else, indefinable but tangible, an element of mystery and mysticism. And Glastonbury today perfectly reflects this blend of past, present and future, the known and the unknown, the fact and the legend.

AN EARLY view of the Market Cross with the tower of St John's in the background. The street is very quiet and the cart, its driver and the two or three curious onlookers seem to have been posed for the photographer.

THE TRIBUNAL in the High Street. Now the home of a museum, it was originally a court which dispensed justice on behalf of the Abbot to the people of the Twelve Hides which came under his jurisdiction. It was built in the 15th century with a timber front – Abbot Bere added the stone front in 1500.

GLASTONBURY LANDMARKS

NO TOWN stands still, and Glastonbury today has its share of twentieth century trappings – new houses and supermarkets and the like. But at the heart of the town are buildings that have witnessed history unfolding throughout the centuries, buildings that are very much a part of the Glastonbury story, past, present and future.

One of Glastonbury's oldest buildings, the Tribunal in the High Street, dates back to the fifteenth century but nowadays houses a museum. It was here that the court was held, dispensing justice on behalf of the Abbot to those who lived within the Twelve Hides that came under his jurisdiction. Originally it was timber-fronted; Abbot Beare commissioned the stone front with its mullion windows in 1500. There are also some Elizabethan additions. The interior of the Tribunal has been lovingly restored with fine examples of period fireplaces, panelling and beams. The exhibits include some outstanding Iron Age artefacts: a splendid dug-out boat fashioned from a single tree trunk, a collection of findings from the Glastonbury Lake Village and the Glastonbury Bowl made of natural bronze, beautiful in its simplicity and arguably the Tribunal's greatest treasure.

A little further down the High Street is the George and Pilgrim, which has provided food and drink and accommodation for visitors to Glastonbury for centuries. One of the few pre-Reformation inns in England, it is not known exactly how old it is. We do know it was rebuilt in 1455 by Abbot Selwood and the frontage has hardly changed since then. It is regarded as a very fine example of stone panelled design, with the majority of the panels containing windows. Over the door are three square panels, two of which are decorated with the coat of arms of the Abbey and of Edward IV. The third is blank, but may well have shown the white rose of York, tactfully removed when Henry VII came to the throne. Inside, the inn is full of character, with beamed ceilings, a huge fireplace lined with Delft tiles and dark oak furniture. The patrons who enjoy its hospitality are continuing a tradition that has lasted centuries.

The parish church of St John is also to be found in the High Street. It dates back to Norman times, although it was almost entirely built during the fifteenth century. The tower, completed in 1475, is particularly fine with three stages and a crown. The interior is designed to give a feeling of light and space – Leland described it in 1534 as 'a fair and litesome church' – and like any well-loved church it still contains some original features such as the glass in the side windows of the sanctuary which is fifteenth century.

In the churchyard in front of St John's stood one of the famous Glastonbury Thorns, and indeed it was from this one that for many years sprigs were cut each Christmas and sent to the Queen and the Queen Mother. Sadly, the tree had to be cut down early in 1992, but another, younger, specimen had been planted elsewhere in the churchyard and will take its place.

Another place well worth a visit is the Abbey Museum which is to be found in the Abbey Gatehouse. This building, which faces on to Magdalene Street, dates back to about 1500 and has in its time been used as an inn. But it was originally the main entrance to the Abbey and it is very fitting that it should now house a collection of relics from the Abbey, including some pieces of carved stone which give a tantalising hint of how beautiful the Abbey must have been. There is also an excellent scale model of the Abbey which illustrates the sheer size and grandeur of the Great Church.

The Pump House is also in Magdalene Street, its classical style reflecting the fashion of the day when it was built in 1750, after a man called Matthew Chancellor had claimed the waters of the Chalice Well had healing properties, a claim which prompted thousands of visitors to flock to Glastonbury. The Pump House is now a private residence.

A little further along the road are the Almshouses of St Mary Magdalene, together with a chapel. This is very ancient, dating back to about 1270 when Abbot Michael of Amesbury founded St Mary's

THE GEORGE and Pilgrims Hotel which has provided food, drink and accommodation for visitors to Glastonbury for centuries. It was rebuilt by Abbot Selwood between 1455 and 1475. The three shields above the door show the arms of the Abbey and of Edward IV, the third is blank.

d Abbeygate House (Red Lion) Glastonbury.

THIS POSTCARD, sent in 1908, shows the Abbey gatehouse when it was an inn. It now houses a small museum dedicated to the Abbey.

Hospital with the chapel at the east end. There is some disagreement over the origin of the almshouses; one school of thought believes that in the fourteenth century the roof was removed from the hospital and the cubicles either side converted into tiny cottages, another theory is that the two rows of almshouses were built within the walls of the hospital in the sixteenth century. In any event, one row was demolished in 1958 – hard to credit that such architectural treasures could have been demolished so recently, but throughout the country many ancient buildings which had survived for centuries were lost in the 50s and 60s. Happily, the other row remains and the chapel with its barrel roof and bell-cote was fully restored – ironically just ten years later in 1968, demonstrating the shift in understanding of the importance of these historic buildings.

On the far side of the Abbey grounds, the Abbey Barn has found a new role as home to the Rural Life Museum. A century ago the barn was *'so cloaked in walls and bushes that but a small part of it may be seen'*

THE ABBEY Barn, which now contains the Rural Life Museum with exhibits and displays depicting life in the 19th and early 20th centuries. The barn was built in the 14th century as the storehouse for the Abbey. There are some fine stone carvings including the carved roundel of St Mark above the entrance porch. Inside, two-tier cruck frames support the roof. Local crafts such as cider-making, butter-making, basket-making and smocking are among the museum displays and a cheese room has been reconstructed in the cellar.

THE MARKET Cross, at the junction of High Street and Magdalen Street was built in 1846 and replaced a larger, earlier cross which was pulled down in 1803. Market crosses declared the authority of the market and fulfilled a number of functions.

◄ *THE ABBEY Barn roof with its two tiers of supporting beams.*

91

but it has been restored and roofed in stone and was opened to the public in 1978. It is dedicated to life in the nineteenth and early twentieth centuries and includes a series of displays which follow the life of a farm worker, complete with tropical rooms and settings. Local crafts such as peat digging, willow cutting and cider making are featured and rural life in Somerset a hundred years ago is perfectly recaptured.

Not far from the Abbey Barn in Chilkwell Street are the Chalice Well Gardens. The legend of the Chalice Well is told in another part of this book; suffice to say that many people believe the gardens with their beauty and tranquil atmosphere should be part of every visit to Glastonbury.

In addition to these places of interest – and the list is not intended to be exhaustive – there are a number of events which take place in Glastonbury every year. As befits a town whose history is so steeped in Christianity there are two important annual pilgrimages. The Church of England pilgrimage to the Abbey usually takes place on the last Saturday in June, with the Roman Catholic one following the next day. The Glastonbury Tor Fair can trace its origins back through the centuries – in 1243 Henry III granted an annual six-day fair at Michelmas thereby extending the event from two days. And Glastonbury is part of the famous circuit of Somerset Carnivals, a modern day tradition featuring a parade of brightly lit floats and involving a good deal of local rivalry for the coveted prizes. Glastonbury Carnival takes place on the second or third Saturday of November.

Of course, other towns have fine historic buildings and strong traditions. There are towns that are bigger, prettier and richer than Glastonbury. But what other town can offer such diversity, such wealth of history, legend and myth, combined with a sense of anticipation of a New Age? This is the essence of Glastonbury and this surely makes Glastonbury unique.

MORE BOSSINEY BOOKS ...

ABOUT EXMOOR
by Polly Lloyd
'It is a cameo to be treasured,' *says Polly Lloyd who takes us on a reflective tour of this timeless corner of England.*   Book Journal

STRANGE TALES OF THE SOUTH WEST
by Ronnie Hoyle
The South West is a natural breeding ground for strange tales. Well-known Westcountry journalist Ronnie Hoyle in his debut for Bossiney confirms this eerie fact.

KING ARTHUR IN THE WEST
by Felicity Young & Michael Williams
'*. . . brings together many of the strands in an exploration which takes them from Tintagel Castle and the Great Halls to Dunster and Dozmary, Glastonbury and so many other centres.*'   The Western Morning News

LEGENDS OF SOMERSET
by Sally Jones
65 photographs and drawings
Sally Jones travels across rich legendary landscapes. Words, drawings and photographs all combine to evoke a spirit of adventure.
'*On the misty lands of the Somerset plain – as Sally Jones makes clear – history, legend and fantasy are inextricably mixed.*'
                    Dan Lees, The Western Daily Express

KING ARTHUR COUNTRY in CORNWALL
by Brenda Duxbury, Michael Williams and Colin Wilson
An exploration in words and pictures of Arthurian sites in Cornwall and Scilly.

WESTCOUNTRY HAUNTINGS
by Peter Underwood
'The Westcountry offers ... just about every kind of ghostly manifestation ...' *writes Peter Underwood, President of the Ghost Club.* '*... a chilling look at hauntings from Bristol to Cornwall ... many of the accounts appear for the first time.*'
                    David Henderson, The Cornish Guardian

MORE BOSSINEY BOOKS . . .

KING ARTHUR IN SOMERSET
Rosemary Clinch & Michael Williams
A grand tour of Arthurian locations in Somerset. Many specially commissioned photographs and drawings.

STRANGE SOMERSET STORIES
Introduced by David Foot
UFOs, ley lines, murder, a self-styled Messiah, curiosities, hauntings and psycho-expansion are all featured.

GHOSTLY ENCOUNTERS
by Peter Underwood

GHOSTS & PHANTOMS of the WEST
by Peter Underwood

We shall be pleased to send you our catalogue giving full details of our growing list of titles for Devon, Cornwall, Dorset, Somerset and Wiltshire and forthcoming publications. If you have difficulty in obtaining our titles, write direct to Bossiney Books, Land's End, St Teath, Bodmin, Cornwall.